Messages To My Son

Messages To My Son

Grandma's Secret Scientific Recipe
for a
Happy and Rewarding Life

Fanny Webb

A Penny Trail Press Publication

MESSAGES TO MY SON
by Fanny Webb

Copyright 2008 by Penny Trail Press, LLC

Published in the United States by
Penny Trail Press
P. O. Box 2712
Virginia Beach, VA 23450

Cover design by Cathi Stevenson

1st printing, November 2008
2nd printing, May 2009
10 9 8 7 6 5 4 3 2

All rights reserved, including but not limited to the right to reproduce this work in whole or in part in any form whatsoever; the right to store this material in or introduce it into a retrieval system; and the right to transmit this material in any form by any electronic, mechanical, photocopying, recording or other means without the express prior written permission of the copyright owner and the publisher of this book, except as may be expressly permitted by the 1976 Copyright Act.

ISBN 13: 978-0-9822161-0-1
ISBN 10: 0-9822161-0-6

PUBLISHER'S NOTE:
It is illegal and punishable by law to engage in the scanning, uploading, and/or distribution of this book through the Internet or any other means without the express written permission of the publisher. Please respect the author's rights and do not participate in or encourage piracy of copyrighted materials.

A discounted rate is available on the purchase of 10 or more copies of single titles. For details, please contact the Marketing Director, Penny Trail Press LLC, P. O. Box 2712, Virginia Beach, VA 23450-2712; or visit us online at www.pennytrailpress.com, email: info@pennytrailpress.com.

A Penny Trail Press Publication

Dedication

For my beautiful niece, Lydia,
whose trail of pennies led me to this place.

Contents

Introduction 1
Chapter 1. If I Knew Then What I Know Now 5
Chapter 2. Your Ego is Your Worst Enemy 9
Chapter 3. Karma is Real 13
Chapter 4. Parenting Basics 17
    Respect her 19
    Acknowledge her 25
    Know your time is limited; be with her 26
    Read to her 28
    Let her do it 29
    Choose child care with care 29
    Give her the gift of faith 33
    Nurture an advanced child 34
    Honor your role 35
    Administer proper nutrition 36
    Build memories 38
    Remember family history 38
Chapter 5. Money: How Much is Enough? 41
Chapter 6. Morality is More than Just a Word 45
Chapter 7. Alcohol and Drugs: Beyond the Hype 49
Chapter 8. Choose Your Friends Wisely 53
Chapter 9. The Art and Science of Life 59
Chapter 10. Love Your Work 67
Chapter 11. The Power of Church 73
Chapter 12. Generate Your Own Wisdom 77
Chapter 13. Choose Your Mate Wisely 83
Chapter 14. Knowledge is Power; More is Better 87
Chapter 15. Don't Ever Stop Learning 91
Chapter 16. Only You Can Take Care of You 95
Chapter 17. Charity and Common Sense 99
Chapter 18. Don't Believe Everything You Read 101
Chapter 19. Map Your Spiritual Journey 105
Chapter 20. Pursue Your Life's Purpose 109
Chapter 21. It's All About Me 113
Chapter 22. Keep Your Goat Hidden 119
Chapter 23. Be True To Yourself 121
About the Author 125

Messages to My Son

Introduction

As I was growing up, my parents moved through what I, from my youthful perspective, took to be the standard stages of parenthood. They were all-knowing and perfect during my infancy and early childhood. Then, about the time I reached adolescence, their wisdom suddenly disappeared, replaced by an appalling lack of understanding and sympathy with my predicament. This disconnection, I'm sad to say, persisted throughout my teen years and didn't improve until I was a young adult with a child of my own.

Thankfully, just when I needed it most, their wisdom returned to them; I was honored and grateful to tap into it. Even better, their breadth and depth of knowledge seemed to have matured and expanded. Nothing I could come up with, no question, no problem, no dilemma was new to the world. They had seen it all and knew what to do to fix it. What an incredible relief to have a living, breathing set of life instructors right there at my fingertips.

Okay, stop the music! That's a crock. Although it's true my parents were an endless wealth of valuable information, I was a hard-headed know-it-all who wouldn't listen to good advice from those who offered it. There. I said it. That admission leads me to the point of this book.

Ideally, wisdom is conveyed through the ages, from generation to generation, from parent to child. Given the number of generations that have come and gone since the dawn of man, we should be a blindingly brilliant civilization. So why aren't we? The problem lies in the communication channels that run between teacher and student; some inexplicable blockage, some mysterious white noise, invariably occurs at the onset of the student's adolescence. Small scraps of knowledge manage to seep through, but much is lost to the static.

Introduction

The rest of it must be re-learned the hard way by each successive generation.

So here am I, bursting with the knowledge my parents managed to impart to me, despite my stubbornness, combined with what I've learned on my own over the years. Hmm, what to do with all this wisdom?

The pages that follow contain my ramblings about life. Some are practical, some are theoretical, some are metaphysical. You will probably point out that some of the points I make are restatements of the obvious. You will be absolutely right. But since what's obvious to one reader might be a revelation to another, please bear with me. Let's make this simple deal with each other: You take what makes sense to you and leave the rest for another day. If all goes according to plan, what you leave behind today will catch up with you later.

Oh, and before I give the wrong impression, I want to admit I haven't necessarily lived my life according to these principles. Your grandfather, a spiritual leader, often maintained with his contagious chuckle, "Reformed drunks make the best preachers." I don't have the distinction of being a reformed drunk, but

I have learned much of what I've written about from my own experience and, in my case, the experience was sometimes painful. By the same token, I can't take credit for making all of the mistakes discussed here. I did, in fact, manage to do a few things right. I've encountered many people in my travels through life, some wise and some not so wise, who were kind enough to save me a few hard knocks by teaching me some of my most valuable lessons.

Everyone has something to teach. And everyone has something to learn.

Chapter 1.
If I Knew Then What I Know Now

The members of every generation think their parents are old-fashioned. It's the term we, as children, use to justify our actions and explain why our parents' ways are wrong. In their defense, each new generation sees their predecessors' mistakes and strives to avoid making those same ones. Rightfully so. There are plenty of other mistakes yet to be made and precious little time in which to make them all.

Unfortunately, this reasoning fails to consider that, in most cases, the advice offered by your elders has been corrected to integrate lessons learned along the way. We aren't trying to tell you what to do just to hear ourselves talk. Okay, maybe some of us are. Maybe some of us are even attempting to relive our lives through our children. It's immaterial. Your challenge is to listen for the wisdom amid the static, leverage what we've learned, use it as the foundation for your life, and build upon it. Don't waste time reinventing the wheel; it doesn't need to be any rounder than it already is. Think of it this way: Do you really want to be limited to the same plateaus we've reached? We want more for you. You should want more for yourself, too.

If I knew then what I know now... every generation sings that same tired refrain, and I'm singing right along with them. You want to live your own life; that's understandable and right. It's your life and only you can or should be in charge of it. There will be times—many, many times—when you won't want to hear what we say. You want to do what you want to do and you don't want to hear why it's not a good idea to do it. Or you won't want to do what you don't want to do and you won't want to hear why it would be a good idea to do it. I know. Believe me, I know. Those are the times you must put aside your ego and give fair consideration to the voice of experience. If you can find a way to do this, you will attain heights of personal and professional satisfaction you can't imagine. Not only can you amass an overabundance of material things, but you can find happiness and peace and all those wonderful things that seem, right now and to so many people, to be entirely unattainable.

I'm not claiming we, the older generation, have superior intelligence. What we have are memories (many of them fading, so you'd better listen quickly and carefully) and first-hand experience. We've been there. We've made the mistakes you're going to have the opportunity to encounter and some of us learned from some of those mistakes. It's your choice. You can listen to the voice of experience and avoid the mistake or you can ignore us, listen to your ego, follow the same path we followed, and end up having learned for yourself exactly what we tried to tell you before you started. Do yourself a favor and listen. Your ego will still be there tomorrow but your elders may not be.

Chapter 2.

Your Ego is Your Worst Enemy

No matter how well-adjusted you are, your beloved ego is probably your worst enemy. Like a little devil sitting on your shoulder, it whispers in your ear. It tells you to be offended by the other person's words and deeds. It tells you to spend money and indulge yourself with unnecessary trappings of success. It tells you to say and do things to puff yourself up so you appear bigger and better to yourself and others.

Someone with a healthy self-image is fairly safe from the fallout generated by the antics of his ego. If your opinion of yourself is off kilter, your ego is going to wreak havoc.

If your self-esteem is low, your ego will allow you to tolerate and even attract belittling and abuse from others. You won't follow through on your dreams or protect what's yours. Your ego will convince you that everyone else is smarter, better-looking, and more deserving than you. The depressed ego resists self-awareness. A person with a depressed ego doesn't think he has ego issues because, in his opinion, he really *is* inferior to everyone else.

If your self-esteem is inflated, your ego will amuse others with its conceits; at its worst, it could spur you to harm others. Your inflated ego will convince you that you are smarter, better looking, and more deserving than anyone else—just what the depressed ego sees in everyone else. Like the depressed ego, the larger-than-life ego resists self-awareness. A person with an inflated ego doesn't think he has ego issues because, in his opinion, he really *is* better than everyone else.

If you have low self-esteem, there's good news. If your self-esteem is over-inflated, this same news, should you choose to believe it, won't be so welcome. Here it comes. Are you ready? *You are neither better than nor less than the person standing next to you.*

What, don't you believe me? You think you're better than the person next to you because he's prone to violence and you're not. That makes you better, right? What about your tendency to gossip? He doesn't gossip; he just punches the people he doesn't like. Both traits harm others. Who's to say which is worse? The person you gossip about may prefer a black eye to having his reputation ruined. Just because there are legal consequences to punching someone but not to gossiping about someone doesn't mean one is morally better (or less bad) than the other.

I'm not trying to quash your healthy self-esteem or further deflate your low self-esteem. You know yourself better than I do. Be honest with yourself. If you honestly think you're a horrible person because you gossip, now is the time to turn that trend around. Acknowledge and celebrate your positive traits. Yes, you do have them. Consider the person standing next to you; you should be able to identify something you do better than him, even if it's just the way you appreciate a sunny day. You're pretty awesome, actually.

The plain truth is that we are all a mixed bag of positive and negative traits. Our mission in life is to accentuate the positive and eliminate the negative. It's a tricky balancing act. Some days you'll balance the teacups well; other days, they'll come crashing down. You may think you've banished a particular tendency for good, only to have it resurface when you least expect it. Don't despair. Try again. Keep trying. In the end, if you keep trying, you'll reach the finish line with more positives than negatives, and you will have won the game of Life.

Chapter 3.
Karma is Real

Yep, Karma is real. Whether it's a result of your conscience, the spirit world, or some invisible law of cause and effect, John Lennon was right—it's gonna get you. It's all about the Golden Rule. Remember that? "Do unto others as you would have them do unto you." There's a very practical reason for observing the Golden Rule. Whatever you do unto others is going to come back to you eventually. It's all one big circle.

Let's use the gossip example again. Gossip is a widespread practice and not generally considered a serious character flaw. Do you have an urge to spread some gossip about that guy who angered you? If you give in to the impulse, expect someone to do the same (but worse) to you later. You won't know when, and in keeping with Murphy's Law, it will probably be at the least convenient time in your life. As sure as the winds blow and the tides roll, it will happen. And when it does, you're going to flash back to this moment and remember the words you are reading right now.

The converse is also true. Treat everyone with kindness, generosity, and charity and you will attract those same things to yourself. I know, you don't believe me. You're thinking, "Sure. Yeah. Whatever. You're just saying that to trick me into being a nice person." Why risk it? Do yourself a favor. The next time you're having a bad spell and suspect the dark clouds that have been following you around are never going to clear, think about how you've treated others in the past. I'll bet you'll come up with an irony directly related to your current situation.

We human beings are a conceited species. We tell ourselves we're pretty smart because we've figured out the laws of physics and nature. We've sent men to the moon and brought them back safely. We've developed medicines to cure many of the most awful diseases. But even with the awareness of how these natural laws relate to outer space as well as inner space, we still have trouble accepting that natural laws govern our mundane, earthbound lives, too.

Newton's Third Law of Motion states that, for every action, there is an *equal* and *opposite* reaction. That's Karma at the universe's level. Have you ever heard the quip, "No good deed goes unpunished"? Examine the deed. You will likely notice something that makes you go "Hmmm…" Maybe the deed was done in a spirit of selfishness and ego rather than one of love and compassion; or maybe the "punishment" resembles a not-so-good deed the doer performed in the past. Payback, if you will. Be assured, if you *give* from your heart, offer help out of kindness, you will *receive* help and kindness when you are in need. That's Karma at the human level.

The Golden Rule is much more than a mantra taught to kindergarteners. It is a real and absolute law of nature. Respect it. Follow it, even though doing so may be difficult. Few have perfected the art of living a completely positive, giving, and egoless life. At least no one I know has achieved that goal. I certainly haven't lived perfectly. Despite that, don't, not even for one little second, doubt the Golden Rule is a law of nature. If your actions are harmful to another, expect harm to return to you. If your actions are beneficial to others, expect benefits to return to you. And we all shine on.

I realize that, on some days, this prescription to follow the Golden Rule is going to be a very hard pill to swallow. You'll see people treating others badly, cheating, lying, stealing, and appearing to prosper from their mistreatment of others. You, on the other hand, treat people fairly and are truthful and honest, but you're treated with disrespect and have trouble making ends meet. What's up with that?

I think you know what I'm going to say. First, don't concern yourself with those others. Their actions will return to them as surely as yours will return to you. As for your current circumstances, look back on the thoughts and actions of your past. Something you thought or did in your past triggered today's circumstances. The sooner you accept responsibility for your situation and start spreading the love, the sooner you can create a wonderful future for yourself. Just because others spit in the face of Karma doesn't mean you should. You know better.

Chapter 4.
Parenting Basics

The most important job any man or woman can have, parent or not, is to nurture the new generation into productive, aware, happy, healthy, and balanced adults. Parenting isn't easy, but it *can* be simplified. Each time you look into the face of a toddler, simply remind yourself that the world of your old age is in the hands of this small person. Each time you look into the face of an adolescent, remind yourself that this individual will be in charge during your twilight years of retirement. It's in your best interests to do all you can to contribute to the psychological well-being of these children. It's like the Golden Rule, but targeted specifically to the treatment of children.

Messages to My Son

The frightening thing about becoming a parent for the first time is that you embark on perhaps the most important job of your life with little or no training. Sure, there are plenty of books written on the subject—a great number of them authored by highly qualified professionals and some by quacks, and more continue to be written every day. Read them; most of them won't hurt you or your child, as long as you apply some common sense. The more you read, the better prepared you are, but understand that no amount of reading can substitute for the parenting experience itself. In other words, no matter how many books you read, it doesn't count unless you put into practice what you learn.

The first rule of parenting is this: Don't raise your child as I raised you just because that's how you were raised. I didn't know what I was doing. I was inexperienced and fumbling through parenthood as best I could. I loved you with an intensity I had never before felt, and I tried so very hard to do what was in your best interests at all times. Unfortunately, my idea of what was in your best interests might not have been entirely accurate at all times. My mother, your grandmother, offered advice and, just as I know you will do--or not do--in your turn, I didn't always accept and apply it. I thought I knew best, as if the act of giving birth endowed me with a sudden superior knowledge. Today, I can look back and understand she was trying to convey to me the wisdom she had accumulated through her experiences of parenting four daughters.

Now it's my turn. You taught me many things as we traveled together along the bumpy roads of your youth and it's time for me to share my lessons from those experiences with you. The suggestions I make here are only a few of the things I see as having great impact on the adult a child will become, but they are a good place to start.

Respect her. Let's start with a basic point that I, like many parents, had trouble internalizing. We don't own our children. Your daughter isn't a thing, a possession, or a puppy. She's a person, a very small person. Treat her like one. Show her the respect any person deserves, the respect you want others to show to you.

That doesn't mean you should allow her to get away with childish bad behavior, any more than society should allow you to get away with adult bad behavior.

The goal is not to force her to bend to your will but to protect and guide her and teach her to live a healthy, safe, and loving existence. Sure, you can bully her; you're bigger than she is and you can make her do most anything. But don't forget about Karma. What will it cost you if you force her to behave a certain way?

Nearly every adult carries some memory of our childhood that makes us hurt. Sometimes that memory is accurate, often times it's colored and skewed from many years of resentment. Do you want your daughter to associate that sort of memory with you? How will you feel when she's 16 years old and an anorexic or a cutter—or worse? You won't want to think it's because of anything you did. But guess what? You'll always wonder. For the rest of your life, the thought that you may have contributed to her pain will nag at you.

I'm not suggesting you tiptoe on eggshells and let her get away with unacceptable behavior because you're afraid she'll inflict damage on herself later if you don't let her have her way now. I'm suggesting you tactfully and intelligently guide her along a safer path. Encourage her with rewards, perhaps, to behave in a desired manner. She'll do just about anything for your approval, assuming you haven't destroyed her desire for your approval by placing unreasonable demands and restrictions on her. Just love her.

Show her by example how to behave. If she's throwing tantrums, there's probably a reason for it. That sort of behavior got her attention, good or bad, in the past. Ignore the tantrum. Don't show anger or respond to her tantrum with a tantrum of your own. If you want to remove her from your presence while she's throwing the tantrum, that's fine. It's a very good idea, actually, but do it without shouting or anger. That sort of bad behavior on your part rewards the tantrum by giving her the attention she's courting and, believe me, you can't teach her not to shout at you by shouting at her. Just remove her from the room calmly, lovingly, and with understanding. Tell her you aren't interested in witnessing her tantrum but she can come out to be with you when she's regained her composure. You will be amazed at how quickly her fury dissipates when there's no one around to react to it. And your actions will teach her self-control, which she will need later in life.

I remember learning this lesson when I was small, maybe three or four years old. My parents had to go out of town unexpectedly for my uncle's funeral. I had never before spent time without my mother. My parents left us, my two sisters and me, in the care of our grandmother and her sister, my great aunt.

Great Aunt Lela had never been married and spent most of her life as the house guest of one relative or another. She maintained a visitation circuit among the various relatives, so we saw her once in a while, but we didn't know her well. Grandma loved us, but she was rather eccentric. Let's just say that being left in Grandma's care did not equate to open season on the cookie jar.

I was frightened and emotionally devastated at what I perceived to be abandonment by my mother. I threw myself on my bed and began to wail. I don't recall being a big fan of melodrama, but anyone witnessing my behavior that afternoon would have thought otherwise. Mind you, I wasn't doing it because I thought it would bring my mother back. There was no practical reason for the tantrum. I was hurting from the pain of separation and this was how that hurt expressed itself. Everyone, including the neighbors, apparently, needed to know how deeply I had been wronged.

Great Aunt Lela came in to my room a couple of times and attempted to comfort and distract me, but I wanted none of her ministrations. With each of her unsolicited visits, I cried louder. Then she stopped coming in. To my horror, I noticed my cries were subsiding against my will! Even at that youthful age, I had a well-developed stubborn streak and when I realized my volume was fading (and so was the attention), I cranked it back up. Great Aunt Lela still didn't return to commiserate with me or try to console me. Finally, it dawned on me that my keening sobs weren't going to change anything.

I wiped my tears with the back of my hand and BoBo—my trusty stuffed bear—and I ventured out of my little sanctuary to see where everybody was. Great Aunt Lela and Grandma acted as if nothing had happened. They and my siblings accepted me into the family circle without commenting on my previous awful behavior. They didn't rush to hug me and apologize for ignoring me. They didn't treat me with anger or scold me. They just brought me back into the family group with love and respect, as if I had never taken myself out of their protective circle in the first place.

I have often wondered, since then, if they discussed or planned their response or if it truly was the non-event they represented it to be. Certainly it was not a non-event to me. Obviously not, as I've carried the memory for half a century. The lesson my four-year-old self taught me is plain: Respect her feelings. Regardless of whether you suspect she's trying to manipulate you, her feelings are genuine. Certainly don't give in to unreasonable behavior, but do respect her right to exhibit it now and then. This isn't about you; it's about her. She's learning. Your job is to help her to learn the right things.

Remember the Golden Rule? It applies to children as well as to adults. Treat your child—any child, for that matter—as you would like to be treated. Teach her now that she is worthy of respect so she won't accept disrespectful treatment from others when she's older. You do that by giving her respect. An added benefit to your guidance: give her respect and she'll respect you in return.

Stubbornness in a child isn't always a bad thing. Being the caretaker of a willful child may not be an entirely comfortable role, but the more backbone and determination a child has, the more likely she is to succeed as an adult. Encourage and preserve that quality in her. Of course, it must be shaped and guided. Just don't destroy it in the process of redirecting it. Her stick-to-it-iveness will contribute to a person who will make you proud some day.

Acknowledge her. This part of parenting is so obvious it should go without saying, but sadly many parents overlook it. Acknowledge your child when she speaks to you. I can't tell you how disturbed I feel when I see a child attempt to speak to her parents and receive no response at all. It appears as though the parent has tuned out the child. The most important person in her world—her parent—is treating her as if she is invisible. Then, when the child repeats herself, perhaps more loudly or with near-tantrum antics in a frustrated attempt to make herself recognizable as a living being, the parent snaps at her to be quiet.

Is it any wonder these children grow up with self-image issues? If it isn't a convenient time to talk to your child—and those times should be few and far between—at least respond to her and tell her you can't talk to her right now but you'll be with her in a moment.

She'll appreciate the consideration, and so will everyone else within earshot. If your business is going to take a while, excuse yourself long enough to find out if what she needs to say is urgent. Then, when you have completed your business, remember to get back to her. And *listen* to her. Engage in conversation with her. Don't blow it now. She did as you asked; it's your turn to fulfill your emotional contract with her. Show her she will be rewarded for her patience by giving her your *undivided* attention. Don't repeatedly hit her snooze button without ever giving her the chance to speak. That, my son, is a grave mistake. How would you react to someone who did that to you? So don't put her on pause and forget to resume your conversation with her.

Toys and television can entertain her, but they don't give her the love and comfort she must receive in order to move confidently through life. She needs your attention. She needs you to be present physically *and* emotionally. Respond to her presence. Answer her questions. Have conversations with her. Discuss things that interest her. She is a person.

Know your time is limited; be with her. Try to always remember that her childhood is a precious and limited time. She will not be with you as a child forever, just as you will not be with her as her parent forever. She will grow quickly and, within a few years, she won't want to spend time with you at all. Still later, she won't be able to spend time with you as she becomes occupied with the demands of her busy adult life. Now is your best opportunity to spend time with this miracle you created.

Teach her with love and compassion, give her the benefit of the doubt. Just be with her. There are times when she needs to simply be in your space. No words are necessary. No teaching is required. She needs nothing more than to be in the same room, on the same sofa or at the same table with you, just to know you're there. That's a difficult "simple" task for us as parents. Our lives are so busy and there's always so much to do.

She needs to be held sometimes, and to know that you love her. It's not that she needs to always be told that you love her, although that's good, too, but she needs to feel that you love her. This can only be communicated through stillness and patient quiet. Look into her face, let her study yours. Let her see and experience your tenderness—the side of yourself you won't let almost anyone else see. She needs to know it's there. Later, when she's a teenager, you can pretend you were never a softie and it never happened. But for now, she needs it.

Read to her. No matter what your own educational background might be, if you can read, you have the power to turbo-boost your child's intelligence level. All you have to do is spend 10 minutes at night reading a bedtime story to her before she goes to sleep. Before you know it, she'll be reading to you. This one is especially powerful because it combines *being* with your child, *acknowledging* your child, *showing tenderness* to your child, and lots of other good stuff, with teaching her the joy of reading, learning, and imagination.

Reading is one of the most effective tools a parent has. It wouldn't surprise me if some expert discovered it is *the* most effective tool a parent has. Just do it. An infant won't care whether you're reading her the sports page or a fairy tale, as long as your tone is gentle and you are nurturing her. I know it's challenging to squeeze the day's current demands into a 24-hour period without adding this extra task, but don't think of it as a chore, because it isn't. It isn't even a nonnegotiable activity, like brushing your teeth and showering. It's a pleasure. Read to your child. And, no, letting her watch television or a movie before bedtime is not an acceptable substitute. Educational television has its place, but it does not and should not take *your* place with your child and some reading material.

Let her do it. Speaking of teeth-brushing, allow her to do things for herself. Sure, you can do it for her more quickly and better than she can do it for herself, but how will she learn if she never gets to practice? Let her help with the laundry and the dishes. Give her a broom and let her help sweep. So what if it isn't a perfect job? The value to her self-confidence and feeling of contribution is priceless. And for goodness' sake, don't criticize her efforts! You don't want her to grow up with the conviction that she can't do anything right, do you? On the other hand, you don't want to tell her she did it right when she didn't, because she won't learn that way. You can, however, praise her efforts and show her how to do it better next time.

Choose child care with care. Ah, the good ol' days, when one parent's paycheck (assuming there were two parents) could support the whole family. These days, lots of households have only one parent and even those with two parents often can't survive on the income from just one parent. With both parents working outside of the home, there's no alternative: their children must go to a child care facility. If this is the case in your family, turn that non-family-provided child care into a positive experience. Child care is expensive, but this is not the place to look for a bargain. Shop carefully and choose wisely. Look for a setting where the care providers are genuinely interested in developing the children mentally, physically, and emotionally.

Infants need to feel love and to have their physical and emotional needs met efficiently and consistently, regardless of who the caregiver is. The caregiver must hold and cuddle the baby frequently. If you notice the infants in the facility you are visiting are being fed while lying in their cribs or with bottles propped up instead of being held and fed by the caregiver, run away and don't even *think* about leaving your child there.

Beginning in infancy, your child needs to be in a learning environment. Children absorb knowledge like a sponge! Ensure she's in a place where her mind is being challenged in fun and interesting ways.

Your choice between a commercial child care facility with a school-like environment or a small, in-home setting is based on personal preference and, let's face it, financial considerations. Keep in mind that more regulations are placed on commercial facilities, which usually means the caregivers are more closely monitored.

The financial cost of child care in a caregiver's home is almost always less than the cost at a commercial facility, and this makes in-home care quite attractive to many young parents. Be sure you can trust the provider if you choose an in-home facility, especially if she's operating without assistance or with the assistance of a relative.

Some clues that should raise a red flag include a provider who insists on cash-only payments. This provider might be perfectly legitimate, but this behavior could also indicate tax evasion, public assistance fraud or both. Or, to state the obvious, a provider with open sores should cause you to suspect staph infections or worse—MRSA (a virulent and highly communicable infection that can be deadly).

If you find yourself tempted to ask for an impromptu drug test, consider it a sign that this is not the place for your child. Something in your gut is making you distrust this caretaker. Follow your instincts and run, child in tow, elsewhere.

If you can, drop in unexpectedly at different times of the day. If the caregiver won't allow you to visit without prior notice, you have to wonder what she could be hiding.

Definitely ask for references, but keep in mind that if she is not honest to begin with, her references probably won't be, either. I once knew an in-home child care provider who created prior experience out of thin air by listing a fellow in-home child care provider as a reference who was prepared to state she had employed her in her own child care facility.

I can't stress enough the importance of a trustworthy child care provider. Your child, especially when she's too young to talk, is defenseless. It's up to you to keep her safe, even when you aren't around—*especially* when you aren't around. Don't allow anyone to make you feel you're being paranoid or overly protective. Taking care of your child is your job, even if you must occasionally subcontract the work to someone else.

Give her the gift of faith. Take your child to church—or meeting hall or mosque or synagogue or temple—or provide her with some other form of spiritual teaching. This isn't about the physical trappings of the building or what kind of head covering the leader is wearing or not wearing. As your child matures and faces life's ups and downs, she is going to need something to hold on to. A spiritual grounding is a safe haven and a nurturing mindset for children as well as adults. Whether you have religious beliefs or not, don't deprive her. Let her make up her own mind. She can't do that if she isn't exposed to it.

Talk to her about your own beliefs when she's old enough to understand. Give her the tools she requires to investigate and formulate her own spiritual views. This is one of the most precious gifts you have to offer her and it all starts with early exposure to spiritual beliefs.

Nurture an advanced child. Advanced children have learned at an early age to hear, understand and trust their intuitions and to control their energies and focus. This may take the form of academic, artistic or spiritual excellence, or perhaps a combination of the three. In addition to mastering their gifts, advanced children must learn the same lessons all children must learn, how to get on in the world, how to deal with the pettiness and jealousies they will encounter when they begin school. The advanced child manages many responsibilities just tending to her gifts and non-advanced peers can easily drain her, especially as she becomes a teenager. Start now to teach her love and tolerance for the ones who will torment her as she grows. Nurture her gifts.

How do you do that? Of course there's the time honored practice of teaching her that she's special. That's a start, but alone it can cause as much harm as good. If the only thing you teach your child is that she is special, she might grow to think she is more important than others, and this can lead to that pesky inflated ego. By all means, teach her she's special, but temper it with the knowledge that others are special, too. She must know—and you must teach her—that what she is given is for her alone and that those who aren't given the talents she has been given aren't to be despised or even pitied. They are as they are, just as she is as she is. They have their own path to walk; not all are as evolved as she is, while some may be far ahead of her. She must have faith in herself and it is up to you to instill that faith. That's not to say that she won't have a rocky adolescence; that's part of growing up and she likely won't avoid it, but a strong self-image and awareness of the value of the gifts she possesses will go a long way toward helping her through that time.

Teach her about tools such as prayer, meditation, spiritual aids--the minerals of the earth. Make them a natural part of her life and explain to her the fear and skepticism others have for such things is also something to be tolerated, not argued and scorned. Talk to her, talk to her, talk to her. And remember that talking to her also means listening to her.

Honor your role. As she goes through life, she will have many teachers. For now, when she is very young and at the most sensitive point in her learning career, you are her teacher. What you say becomes her truth, one that she will carry with her for the rest of her life. She may later discover that something she learned from you is not so, but she will never fully disbelieve it. You are her sage. Wear that mantle with honor and care.

You will be amazed at how quickly she will internalize the things you teach her. They resonate with her as truth and become part of her being. Be aware of your words and behavior when you are around her. She will learn from what you do as well as what you say, regardless of whether the doing or the saying is directed at her.

Administer proper nutrition. No discussion of child behavior and child rearing would be complete without touching on the subject of mealtimes. So she won't eat her dinner? Big deal. She ate a big lunch and snacked throughout the afternoon. Little ones are busy, too busy to eat.

The goal of mealtimes is to get nutritious foods into her, not to play a stressful power game at the dinner table. Tempt her, make those foods available to her outside of mealtime. Finger foods she can eat on the fly while playing, such as raw vegetables and fruits, count as intake. Even if she isn't eating them while she's sitting down, she's still eating them and that's what counts. If she isn't eating the balanced diet you think she needs despite your best efforts, make sure she gets a daily vitamin. If she gets a balanced diet over a week's time, she's doing great. There's nothing magic about the dinner table. Seek your pediatrician's input on this subject, too.

Don't misunderstand me on this. She certainly should be encouraged to sit at the dinner table to provide a sense of structure and encourage her sense of belonging. But if she chooses to eat carrot sticks at 4:00 p.m. while watching cartoons on television, count it as a success. If you were to keep a list of all she eats during the day, I think you would be amazed at the quantity of food she actually consumes outside of the traditional mealtime hours. Your job is to make sure those snacks are nutritious.

Respect her likes and dislikes. She does need to try different foods and you have every right and the responsibility to ask her to taste things she hasn't tried before. She won't like everything, and foods she doesn't like today may be her favorite flavors next year. Tastes change. You enjoy foods as a grown-up you would never have eaten when you were a child. Praise her attempts to try new things. Some kids actually *love* broccoli. They won't know until they try.

Of course, if she only "likes" junk food and sugar, we have a different set of problems. Try to guide her back to a healthy menu by giving her natural sugars like fruits and yogurts for snacks and desserts.

Little children have little stomachs. Her little body can accommodate only so much food, so make what she does eat count. Don't pile food in front of her at mealtimes with the expectation that she must clean her plate. Small amounts, by your standards, will fill her. If you insist she eat large portions, she may return it to you sooner and less pleasantly than either of you would expect. Trust me on this one.

Build memories. Whatever you're doing, imagine she'll remember it for the rest of her life. How do you want her to remember you? The most fleeting and insignificant moment in your life could very well be a life-changing event in hers. Behave positively. Act kindly. Smile. Have fun.

Remember family history. Never forget that your life did not begin when you were created. Your life began with your father and me, and our lives began with our parents, all the way back to the beginning of time. If there's genetic disease in the family, share that knowledge with your child as soon as she is old enough and mature enough to understand the ramifications of that information. This especially includes a predilection to addiction. If anyone directly contributing to her genetic makeup was an alcoholic or drug addict, tell her about it and explain to her that it means she could be susceptible to addiction. Help her understand it's a disease, not a reflection of character, and give her the advantage of knowing that to experiment with addictive substances is more dangerous to her than it might be to her peers. By the same token, the earlier she knows that heart disease has attacked her family, the earlier she can consciously start living a heart-healthy lifestyle.

The timing of this talk depends on the maturity of the child. A good rule of thumb would be to talk to her about it around the same time you talk to her about sexual activity. Most likely she should be capable of understanding by the time she's twelve. If you are already suffering from a disease, she'll probably have suspicions about it sooner and you should be prepared to discuss it, at some level, before she's old enough to ask you well-formed questions. Feel free to ask your pediatrician for additional guidance. You don't want to scare her, but waiting too long can have disastrous consequences.

Chapter 5.
Money: How Much is Enough?

No matter how much money you make, you'll always want more. This is not to say you will *need* more, but you will *want* more. Do yourself a favor and decide to be satisfied with and grateful for what the money you make today can buy you today. Make a game of it. Money is the opponent whose goal is to make you dissatisfied with your lifestyle. You win when you are happy with what your money can provide for you. Love that broken-down vehicle you're driving; without it, you'd be walking or staying home. Relish the peanut-butter sandwiches you're eating; the alternative could be hunger.

Now I know this one's going to be a little tough to swallow, but stay with me: The happier you are with what you have, the more you will get. It's true. When you become truly happy with and grateful for what you already have, more will come. Here's a little twist to the game, though. If you are wasteful with what you have, the flow to you will be stemmed. Charity is good and that's not what I'm talking about here. I'm talking about wastefulness. Spending a quarter of your weekly earnings for a single meal at an overpriced restaurant or purchasing luxuries when you can't pay for necessities are examples of wastefulness. Spend responsibly, appreciate what you have, and be happy. That's the secret to abundance.

From a practical standpoint, your credit is important in many ways. You need it to obtain a loan. You need it to obtain housing. You can neither rent nor buy a home with bad credit. Your insurance premiums are partially based on your credit report. Some employers look at your credit report to determine reliability. Credit card companies look at your credit report. If your credit score is good, they'll send you a credit card, sometimes unsolicited. Use that card, get into debt—it's way too easy to do—and, all of a sudden, you can't make your payments, or you're late making them, and your good credit isn't so good anymore.

If your credit gets bad enough, the credit card company will cancel your card and ask you to pay the balance all at once, instead of in relatively manageable installments. Now you can't get a loan to repay the credit card because your credit is bad. The cycle becomes a vicious nightmare that could take years, a decade or more, or bankruptcy to fix. Even if you accept a credit card with the intention of paying off the balance in full each month, you will, one day, suddenly realize you don't have enough to pay it off. You'll defer paying off that balance until next month, and then you'll add to the balance by continuing to shop, while the credit card provider is adding to the balance with interest. Next month's bill comes and, no surprise, the balance you couldn't pay last month is even higher. Compound interest means you'll be in debt way over your head, no matter how tall and grown up you are.

The problem is, you almost have to have a credit card these days. You need it to rent a car, reserve airline tickets, make hotel reservations, and more. Yes, you do have to have a credit card, but you don't have to *use* it for everything. Keep it someplace where it's difficult to access to discourage impulse purchases. Get into a mindset that you will use it for nothing except for those absolutely necessary situations such as hotel reservations and car rentals. I recently read about someone who keeps his card in the freezer, frozen inside a block of ice. Before he can use it, he must melt the ice. This gives him time to reflect on whether the purchase is a necessity or a whim. Yes, you probably need a winter coat, but you don't need two of them. Think before you actually buy and you won't have bill collectors calling you at all hours of the day and night.

Chapter 6.
Morality is More Than Just a Word

Morality isn't a vague shoulda-woulda-coulda ivory-tower concept. Morality is a practical how-to-travel-through-life-with-as-little-misery-as-possible roadmap. Take sex, for instance. Depending on who you talk to, the morality means *"Don't have sex until you're married,"* or *"Don't have sex with someone you don't love,"* or *"It's only a physical release, so what's the big deal?"* What I've witnessed over the years leads me to believe that those who think sex is just a physical thing tend to be very unhappy people. Why is that, do you think? Are they unhappy because they have a cavalier attitude about sex, or are they cavalier about sex because they're unhappy? Or does one have absolutely nothing to do with the other?

Casual sex is nothing more than randomly selective copulation with the partner of the moment whose appearance or scent or online message stirs your libido. Make no bones about it, casual sex has led to rampant sexually transmitted diseases, lots and lots of single-parent homes, and children being raised by stepparents, grandparents, and foster care parents.

There's an ancient belief that when you have sex with someone, you give a part of yourself to your partner and in return, her life-force melds with yours. After copulation, you are forever changed, like flour that's been mixed with water and can't be unmixed. Personally, I want to know the person I'm about to meld with is someone I won't mind carrying around with me the rest of my life.

Then there's the corollary, the possibility that melding with one person can create another person—a baby. Once that baby is created, you have a decision to make. Do you keep the baby? If yes, do you marry its co-creator? Whether you marry or not, if you have a baby together, you become connected for life. Do you really want to go through life connected to someone you don't like? Why not prevent the possible situation from unfolding in the first place? Just don't have sex with someone you wouldn't be willing to see every Christmas, birthday, holiday, and weekend for the rest of your life! More importantly, don't have sex with someone whose characteristics you wouldn't want to see recreated in your own child. Genetics is real, you know—and science can prove that one.

Being a single mom is difficult. Being a single father is difficult. Ditto being a stepparent. Being the child of a broken family is unimaginably difficult. Being the grandparent of such a child is difficult. Sure, once born, this child will bring joy and light into the world of all who love her, but the ramifications of the circumstances of her birth can cause her, and those who love her, pain. This widespread suffering could be minimized if men and women would be selective about with whom and under what circumstances they choose to mate.

You might have no intention of spending more than one hot night with the lady of the moment, but many children have been born out of such a union, spawning pain for at least two people—the mother and the child—as well as the father, if he knows about it, the grandparents, and possibly a stepfather. You, the biological father, may never know the child is yours and may never even meet the child, but Karma-wise, you're still on the hook for inflicting the pain. Or you may know the child is yours and spend the next 18 years paying child support, tied to a woman who turns your life into a living nightmare.

Equal and opposite reactions. Could the situation have been avoided? Absolutely. Go way back to the moment your libido was first stirred and be honest with yourself. Did you have any intention whatsoever of spending your life with this person? Even if you felt this could be The One, did you know her well enough to be reasonably certain you could spend your life with her? Avoid all that future suffering. Get to know her first. If she isn't someone you could spend your life with, move on.

Give your child the gift of two loving parents who love each other as much as they love her.

Chapter 7.

Alcohol and Drugs: Beyond the Hype

The subject of alcohol and drugs often explodes into a counter-culture, us-against-them, impassable chasm between the generations. I'm not going to tell you if you abuse alcohol or drugs, you should be sure to pack flameproof garments for your afterlife. But there are plenty of police officers out there who won't hesitate to tell you that, although alcohol is legal, it's not legal to be drunk in public or while operating a vehicle. And while some folks protest that marijuana should be legal, it's not legal in most countries and, if you're caught with it, you're going to court and perhaps to jail. American jails aren't pretty and foreign jails are even less so.

What I am here to tell you is that overindulging in any mind-altering substance has many side effects that derail happiness.

First, it can cause you to violate the "careful who you have sex with" and "attract only good Karma" rules.

Aside from that, there's the damage to your health. If you do it long enough and often enough, it can become an addiction that controls your life.

To these risks to your body, mind and Karma, add the risk to your freedom. This is an indulgence that can cost you your freedom and/or a large chunk of money spent attempting to preserve your freedom.

You already know all this, but here's one I don't hear often: Indulging in alcohol and drugs blocks your spiritual receptors. You can't hear the messages. You don't know the questions. And that isn't just while you're under the influence. I don't know how long it takes to completely clear yourself of the effects of a drink; I just know that even one drink causes me to lose touch with my inner voice for a while. Maybe your inner voice is louder than mine, but you get the picture.

With all of these consequences lined up to pounce on those who abuse alcohol and drugs, why risk it? Are the "benefits" really worth the price?

No, this isn't a counter-culture issue. Indulging in mind-altering substances is risky at best and life-destroying at worst. Maybe you enjoy relaxing at the end of the day with a drink or a joint and you're willing to accept the risks that go with it. It's your decision; no one can make that choice for you. My purpose here is to offer you an informed choice and maybe, just maybe, stimulate that all-important split second of clarity when you realistically and honestly weigh the benefits against the risks to your body, mind, Karma, freedom, bank account and soul and make a conscious decision to guard your future from these consequences.

Chapter 8.
Choose Your Friends Wisely

Choose your friends carefully and then cherish them fiercely. You may have one or perhaps two friends in your lifetime who will stay with you over the years. But for the most part, a friend is not a constant throughout your life. He is there during a particular stage of your life, and as you grow different friends take center stage. This can also be true of family. Although you grow up in a family with brothers and sisters and you continue to see them sporadically throughout the years at various family functions, they may not truly be part of your life. Recognize that, after all is said and done, your life is a solitary journey and your friend's is as well.

Choose friends who sympathize with your beliefs and support your goals. Your friends must believe in what you're trying to accomplish if they are to support you in your struggles.

Never lend money to your friend. This one guideline has been around forever, yet it seems we all have to learn this lesson the hard way. The surest way to end a friendship is by lending money. If you want to help, give the money as a gift and don't expect repayment. If you expect repayment and don't get it, you'll have lost both the money and the friend.

You won't agree with all the opinions and beliefs of any one person. No amount of arguing and debating will ever make that so. Decide to respect the opinions of others—yes, even about politics and religion—and understand that it's okay to disagree. If we were all the same, the world would be a very boring place.

You will have some true friends whose influence will stay with you for a lifetime. These people don't judge you or want anything from you, but simply ask, "What can I do to improve your life?" Okay, so maybe they don't come out and say that, but you know they are there for you, no matter what else is going on in your life, and you are equally there for them. The woman you marry should be such a friend.

Many times we form friendships with people who enjoy a little gossip; I've done it myself, and it's difficult to resist participating in a friend's favorite pasttime. Sometimes the gossip is harmless; sometimes it can be quite hurtful. Just keep in mind that a gossip will talk about you to others as readily as she will talk about others to you. If you find you wouldn't mind being the subject of your friend's gossip, that her tone is entertaining and harmless, your friendship is probably safe. Still, you would be wise to not confide anything in a friend prone to gossip that you wouldn't want broadcast to the community. The way your friends treat their enemies is the way they could eventually treat you. It's only a matter of time and circumstances. If your friend talks unkindly about others, he'll talk unkindly about you at some point, whether you ever know it or not.

A healthy friendship involves give and take on both sides. A friendship in which only one person is giving is not a true friendship, but a parasitic relationship. Periodically, people will enter your life who are takers, always wanting more from you. They're like vampires, draining you of everything they can get from you. What you offer is never enough; they keep coming back asking for more. When they've exhausted you of everything they can get, they move on to find another person to suck dry. They think of people as the source of their supply. This kind of person is not the woman you want to marry, nor is he or she the kind of friend you want to keep. It's easy enough to detach yourself from this kind of person. Stop giving to the person, stop letting the person take from you, and that person will quickly move on to the next victim.

This is not to say you should not practice charity. There are those who, for one reason or another beyond their control, cannot support themselves. Giving gladly, willingly, and freely to those people provides them relief and is good for your soul as well.

Sometimes it's difficult to differentiate between the calculating vampires and the deserving unfortunates. Imagine the public assistance program offices everywhere that face this dilemma on a daily basis! It's especially difficult for a man to see a woman—or worse, a woman with a child—asking for assistance.

If you pay attention to details, you'll see clues. The vampire seems to be between jobs quite often. The vampire doesn't hesitate to ask you to drive her miles out of your way; do this once and you become the vampire's taxi until you finally refuse to be at her beck and call. The vampire appears grateful for your help and tells you what a wonderful friend you are, perhaps claiming to be lost without your help while in the same breath asking for more.

The vampire may or may not offer to reimburse you, but if you accept her offer she'll be ready with a reason why she must "pay you next Tuesday for a hamburger today." It won't matter to her that she's also robbed you of time, which can't be recovered or replaced. Maybe you're noticing things missing from your home after the vampire has visited.

You might notice some sort of dishonesty in the vampire's dealings with other people, perhaps lying to get something she wanted. Remember, vampires and false friends share a common characteristic: even if they don't do so now, eventually, they will treat you as they treat others when it suits their purpose.

Likewise, don't be a parasite on your friends. Just as you must choose your friends carefully, so must your friends choose theirs. Be supportive and believe in your friends. Do unto others as you would have them do unto you. Hmm, that sounds familiar, doesn't it?

Chapter 9.
The Art and Science of Life

If you look closely enough, you'll begin to notice there's a fine line between art and science. Scientific facts are theories we know how to prove. What about those theories we haven't found a way to prove? Are they untrue because we haven't discovered their proofs yet? Bear with me, open your mind, and consider the following.

Electrons and quarks are the fundamental subatomic particles that compose everything that exists now or existed in the past. Odds are good they'll comprise everything in the future, too. You probably learned that in a physics class. If you didn't, you can take my word for it or you can look it up. But it is fact.

Electrons and quarks each have properties that make up their own intelligences. What do they know? The electron knows it's negatively charged. The quark knows how it is charged and how to interact with other quarks to form protons and neutrons. Protons and neutrons know how many up and down quarks construct them, and how to interact with each other and with electrons to form atoms. More facts.

Atoms, in turn, possess the individual intelligences of the electrons, protons, and neutrons that combine to produce them, plus a little more—a collective intelligence formed when these particles merge their separate intelligences. For instance, an atom knows what kind of atom it is, its atomic weight, its electron configuration, its melting point, and its specific gravity.

Atoms combine to make molecules. A molecule inherits the intelligences of the various atoms that formed it, and adds its own collective intelligence. It knows its molecular structure, the type of bonds holding its atoms together, and the energy of those bonds.

And so on and so on. Every little element is part of some bigger something, and those bigger somethings are parts of even bigger somethings. The circle of life gets bigger with every go-round. All science.

Groups of molecules work together to form the organs we call hearts, livers, and brains. Each organ is endowed with its own collective knowledge and those organs unite to form, among other things, systems called human beings.

All human beings are constructed with the same basic ingredients of quarks and electrons, but no two human beings are made in the exact same proportions. The life experiences of a person, or that person's interactions with other entities and environmental factors, further alter the collective intelligence of that person's elements. As a result, each human system has a different intelligence than the system next to it. Simply put, we're all the same *and* we're all different. So far, so good.

Animal systems join with plant systems and mineral systems to create the earth system, just as heart systems and lung systems join with other systems to create the human system. If more complex means more intelligent, does that mean the earth and the universe, which are both infinitely more complex than a single human being, are more intelligent than I am? Do the earth and the universe have the capacity for thought and logic and reasoning and emotion and love? Do they possess some other type of intelligence that we more primitive life forms cannot even imagine?

My heart and liver and lungs all contribute to my intelligence but they don't individually have the intelligence that I, as a system, can boast. Following that reasoning, I contribute my thoughts and emotions to the intelligence of the universe but I don't individually have the intelligence of the universe.

My heart and liver and lungs can benefit from my intelligence as a system in that my thoughts can command my heart to beat more slowly, my lungs to draw air more deeply. I can exercise my body as a system to keep my heart healthy and my muscles strong. Does the universe exercise such control over me? Am I a finger on the hand of the universe? Does the universe possess the superior intelligence to orchestrate the lives of each of its "organs", monitor the needs and desires of each soul, just as I rest my feet when they are tired and soothe my skin when it is chapped? If so, is the universe's attention claimed by the squeaky wheel or is it proactive enough to feel a headache coming on and take preventive measures?

Is the universe sufficiently advanced to hear and respond to the prayers and pleas of the meditative soul? Have I arrived at the conclusion that God is the mind and soul of the universe, the ultimate system of which all matter is a part?

If all this is true, what good would this knowledge do us? It would tell me that to hurt another entity is a larger form of self-mutilation. Do my thoughts direct me to hurt myself? No. Do the thoughts of someone with an unhealthy psyche direct her to hurt herself? Sometimes. What causes that? I believe it boils down to painful thoughts. Someone who has deeply painful thoughts might choose to hurt herself, if only to physically overcome those painful thoughts. What brings those painful thoughts to her? Negative emotions, perhaps generated by negative experiences.

Here's my theory. My thoughts and emotions are formed from the combination of the intelligences contributed by individual parts of me, including the memories of my experiences. If I contribute negative thoughts and emotions to the universe, I am contributing to the universe's pain. If I cause others to contribute negative or painful thoughts to the universe, I am contributing to the universe's pain. Since I am part of that universe, I am causing myself pain. But wait! There's more! Since my loved ones are also part of that universe, my negative thoughts and emotions and the negative thoughts and emotions I generate in others cause pain to my loved ones. Could this explain why bad things happen to good people? Perhaps. If nothing else, it certainly means we are all responsible for each other's well-being.

If we're all part of the same system, might cutting down trees equate to giving the earth a haircut or cutting the grass equate to trimming the universe's sideburns? That would indicate pollution is to the universe as cigarette smoke is to my lungs. Toxic waste dumps become pockets of cancer. What I do to my neighbor, my right hand does to my left hand.

My mind can choose to take care of my body or neglect it, but the more healthy exercise my body gets, the more it craves and the more it demands that my mind make time to care for it. As my body demands attention from me, I demand attention from the universe. When I am passive, I am easily ignored. When I shout my prayers persistently and insistently, I am heard and attended to.

Just as I can tell my lungs to breathe more deeply, so can the universe give me direction. Just as some people can more easily control their heart rate and blood pressure with their thoughts than other people can do, so can some people receive instruction from the universe more easily than others. It's called intuition. Intuition isn't a talent you must be born with. It's a skill that can be developed and strengthened and honed with practice.

So, we are energy and, as such, we vibrate at varying frequencies, according to the activity of our electrons and quarks. If we are energy, then what are thoughts? Are they energy, too? No, they're the potentiometers, the dials, that control our emotions and cause the frequencies of our subatomic particles to vary. They work together, energy and potentiometers.

If my inner being is energy and my thoughts are the potentiometers that tweak my emotions to control my energy's vibration, what controls my thoughts? What turns those dials? Is this where the soul enters the picture? Is the soul not energy? Or is it another form of energy, the higher form, the higher consciousness, the higher self, a part of the universal consciousness that has separated from the whole like a little ball of mercury to become me? That combination of electrons and quarks made up of the same properties as the universal intelligence, the same properties as the other pieces of universal intelligence that form my friends, family, and co-workers and are ready to flow back into the whole whenever the time is right, that's what controls my thoughts, which control my emotions, which control my frequencies.

What does all this mean? The bottom line is this: what I do to myself, I do to you. What I do to you, I do to myself. My thoughts affect you, your thoughts affect me. The basis of the fantasy *Neverending Story*, the children's book written by Michael Ende, was not so far-fetched. The life and health and well-being of the planet and all it supports are affected by the mental health of the humans who inhabit it. The good news is that we are also capable of changing the energy we contribute, through our thoughts.

Chapter 10.
Love Your Work

Do what comes easily to you. If you don't have the underlying attributes needed to be a successful business person, don't try to make a living in business administration. Follow your bliss *and* your talents. Sometimes that means less money. After all, a business owner generally makes more money than the people he hires. Making money is his talent. The satisfaction you will receive from doing what you love and what you're good at will compensate for the more modest standard of living. If you work at a job you don't like *and* you are making very little money doing it, you will be doubly stressed! If you make a lot of money while working at a job you don't like, you'll still be stressed, but you may temporarily be somewhat consoled by the higher income. While it's true the job you love and are good at can also be stress-producing, you'll find you thrive on the same stress that would make you ill if it were derived from work you disliked doing.

You can tolerate a job mismatch for a time by telling yourself you can handle anything for enough money, but you'll eventually realize you've been lying to yourself. Sooner or later, the negatives resulting from doing something you dislike doing, regardless of how well-compensated you might be, will build up to explosive pressure.

Your approach to a career choice can be as simple as a process of elimination or as sophisticated as a career interest test or consultation with a life coach. First, decide what it is you do well and enjoy doing. Is this a salable skill? Consider digging fishing worms? Don't knock it, the bait doesn't crawl into the can all by itself. No, it doesn't pay a lot, but if that's what soothes your soul, maybe there's a living there. Can you open a bait store near a fishing hole? Not business-minded? Can you find a partner who is? Be sure it's a partner you can trust, and follow his advice as far as business is concerned. The point is, don't compound your problems by trying to do or be something you aren't suited for. It might work for a short time, but in the end it will hurt. And what hurts you hurts the universe and me.

My suggestion to anyone unsure about their career choice is to find and take a career interest test, such as the Strong Interpretive Report. These tests are amazingly accurate and are available through the guidance offices of most schools. If you don't have access to a school guidance office, you can probably find them on the Internet for a modest fee.

If you can't find a way to take a career interest test, at least make a list of your strengths and weaknesses. For example, I'm best suited for writing, organizing, and research. These things are obvious to anyone who knows me. My family has a running joke about my lists. Keep in mind, too, that things change. You could be well-suited for dealing with difficult people in your younger years but lose patience for it as you grow older. Did you ever wonder why people switch careers late in life? Perhaps their first career suited them well at the time, but they outgrew it.

That brings me to a good point. What do you do when you outgrow your career? Ideally, you know what you want to do next and prepare yourself for it through education and by researching how to get there from here. If it sneaks up on you, begin preparing for it when you discover it.

Your work doesn't have to rock the world. There's a need for the mundane as well. Don't mistake mundane for unimportant. Don't mistake low pay for not valuable. So what if your talent is for a low-paying occupation? The value is in the doing and if it brings you bliss and you can survive on it, then do it. If you have a yearning for riches, consider combining your talents with a higher-paying approach. Or maybe a yearning for riches is something you can eliminate from your life. Yes, you need to be able to feed, clothe, and house yourself and your dependents, but look at how you spend money. Do you really need that cellular telephone? Would your quality of life plummet if you didn't receive all the premium cable channels?

Can you survive at a high-paying job you dislike and pursue your bliss in your free time? Absolutely. Lots of people do this very thing. You just have to decide for yourself how miserable you are willing to be in order to surround yourself with things you don't really need.

We have learned to consider many things as our birthright that are unnecessary to our happiness and our subsistence. Nobody wants to have to scrimp and scrape to make ends meet and I'm not saying you should aspire to that. But if the choice comes down to doing what you love and scrimping and scraping, or doing something that makes you unhappy and making lots of money—consider scraping.

Chapter 11.
The Power of Church

I grew up going to church because I was given no choice. To me, it was just a torture to be endured on Sunday mornings, something I had to do because that's what good people did. When I was old enough to assert my will—and that was at sixteen years of age—I stopped going.

A funny thing happened a few years later, when I was twenty. I became spiritual. It started very selfishly with a mind training technique, a way I thought I could get what I wanted using the power of my mind. I delved deeper and deeper into the workings of the mind and the mysteries of life. I was fascinated with it but, as a high school graduate, I felt under-educated and not qualified to judge whether the things I read had merit.

I began going to a non-denominational Christian church and found answers there that I never expected. When I meditated, I truly felt I was communicating with God. Soon, though, life interfered with my new-found spirituality and, once again, I stopped going to church. I didn't think being in the church building was a requirement for spirituality; I could talk to God just as easily from the physical comfort of my home.

I had been smoking marijuana regularly for a couple of years and noticed that, when I was high, I couldn't find that place in my mind where I felt connected with God. After a while, I couldn't find my way there even when I wasn't high. I felt I had lost God and it was a terrible loss. I didn't know how to get Him back, and I missed Him.

Now, as I look back on that time with the perspective of distance, I wonder if my loss was the result of not going to church. The value of church doesn't lie entirely in the message delivered by the minister. The delivery of the message generates a collective energy in the congregation, a grateful, expectant energy that emanates out from the building into the world and joins with the energy emanating from the church down the street, which joins with the energy from the churches in the next town and so forth until the vibrations of all the grateful, expectant, meditative, and prayerful beings synchronize to create a healing, soothing, creative energy that acts like a balm on the souls of the participants and non-participants alike and manifests goodness in the world.

All those people reading the *New York Times* in bed on Sunday morning —why do you think this is their favorite time of the week? Yes, it's a time to relax, but they are unknowingly also getting the benefit of the energy produced by the church-goers. You can certainly reap the benefits of spirituality in solitude, but joining with others amplifies the power of your spirituality. Imagine the vibrational frequency that could be attained in the world if we all spent that one hour a week attuning ourselves to God's energy.

Yes, church is a building, but it's not the physical structure so much as the community of souls that congregate there that's important. And it doesn't matter whether the structure is a church, a mosque, a synagogue, a temple, or a tent. Just go to church a few times and see if you don't agree with me on this point. And, if you have one, take your child with you!

Chapter 12.
Generate Your Own Wisdom

As you were growing up I wanted to teach you from a place of wisdom, and I know you will in your turn want to teach your own child from a place of wisdom. But we can't be wise by spending our time going to work, coming home, eating dinner, going to bed, and then doing it all again the next day. We must spend some time in meditation and studying what wise men have said. Wisdom isn't the regurgitation of what others have said through the ages. Collect the ideas of your teachers, internalize the ones that resonate as truth, and weave them together with your own epiphanies to generate your own wisdom. Then you can teach your child from a place of wisdom and you can live your life with joy and purpose.

By now, I hope you're beginning to realize that everything works together. The rules of the game of life are amazingly interconnected and synergistic. A great deal rides on the state of your emotions. Just as your house needs to be cleaned regularly, so does your mind. Mental housekeeping helps keep your thoughts and actions positive, which supports Newton's Third Law of Motion, that for every action, there is an equal and opposite reaction.

The most expedient and effective way to accomplish this mental housecleaning is to allow an objective and trained professional to counsel you through it. Entering mental health counseling is not a sign of weakness. It helps guide you through confusing and painful times when your thoughts may become jumbled and disorganized.

You might point out, astute person that you are, that some people have been in counseling for years and their mental functions continue to be suspect. Well, maybe some people aren't such good housekeepers; maybe they don't put enough elbow grease into the cleaning process. Maybe they have more cobwebs and dark corners than your mind or my mind has. It doesn't matter. Your results reflect your effort.

The act of appearing at a therapist's office and spending an hour with her periodically isn't going to be effective unless you put into practice the things you discover there. It's like going to church. You can take your place in a pew every weekend, but unless you practice the principles during the week, your appearance in church is just for show and those folks whose opinion really matters—your child, for example—will know you're not serious about it.

As an evolved individual, you can go to your special place to find peace of mind. You know, that place deep within your soul where you tap into the wisdom of the ages. Some people have found a direct and infallible way to reach this place, while others are only lucky enough to stumble upon it by accident and not be able to find it again. Most folks have been there at one time or another and the lucky ones can go there at will.

Here's a recipe for finding that place within yourself. It's adapted from an exercise I learned many years ago. It starts with controlling your breathing while in a specific position. Of course, you don't have to be in these positions, but I think the position of your body is key in gaining the full benefit of the exercise, especially if you can't find that special place whenever you want to go there. You can be sitting or lying down.

If you choose to sit, fine. Sit in a chair with your legs uncrossed, feet on the floor, and hands in your lap. If you're lying down, lie flat on your back, legs uncrossed, with your arms at your sides. Once you're in position, close your eyes and take three deep, slow breaths. With each breath, visualize a countdown from three to one, starting with the numeral three. Visualize the numeral in your mind, dress it up, color it, animate it, and focus all your attention on the numeral three as your draw in a deep breath and slowly release it. Do the same for the numeral two. Draw a deep breath, visualize the numeral two, dress it up, color it, animate it, and focus all your attention on the numeral two as you draw in and slowly release your breath. Do the same for numeral one. Then, visualize yourself stepping onto a down escalator. Draw a deep breath and, as you exhale, begin to slowly count down from ten to one. Visualize each number as you count, and time them so you reach the bottom of the escalator when you reach the number one. This will take a period of three or four deep breaths. Now, step off the escalator. See a door. Behind this door is your special place, the place where you can go to feel peaceful, find answers, and talk with the sages deep within your soul.

The more often you visit this place, the easier it will be to get there, and believe me, this is a place you want to know well.

Is there a spirit realm? I believe so, although please don't interpret this as a place where ghosts hang out. I believe the spirit realm is the dimension of collective energies, intelligences and knowledge formed from the contributions of all the individual beings of the universe, and I believe we communicate with this dimension through our thoughts—not just any thought but those thoughts that are totally present, the ones that come out of meditation and are not tainted by past or future. Since our limited understanding usually needs to associate a form with the entity we're communicating with, the concept of spirit guides has arisen. Try it. Close your eyes and imagine having a conversation with a spirit guide—imagine the spirit guide as a person, if it helps. You might think you are forcing the words into his mouth, and maybe you are at first. But then your imagined guide takes on a will of its own and suddenly the thoughts entering your mind come from the spiritual realm. The answers you get are legitimate. The more you practice this, the more legitimate the answers.

Don't know what to do about a situation? Can't make a decision? Ask and listen. You may find yourself doubting the answer, afraid it is just a reflection of your own desires. Make a deal. Require that the answer's manifestation in the physical world have a code. For example, if you feel led to quit your job and you're afraid to do so without one in the hand, require that the new job come to you first, and that you'll know it by some code—say, "Red". When the job with the color red attached to it appears and all other circumstances are right, take it. Practice this enough and you won't require the code, you'll trust your meditative communications and instincts.

Chapter 13.
Choose Your Mate Wisely

As you get older, leading a happy, peaceful life becomes more important to you. Youth enjoys drama and excitement. It thrives on excitement, actually. Trust me when I say that, as you mature, you'll start looking around for ways to attain peaceful happiness. Until you reach that age when you tire of the emotional rollercoaster, though, the words you read here likely won't appeal to you. That's okay. You won't hurt my feelings if you set aside this chapter for now, just promise me you'll return to it before you choose your life companion.

A major factor in your happiness is going to be the mate you choose. The wrong one can make you miserable in the present. Moreover, if you conceive children together, she can haunt you for the rest of your life and—who knows?—maybe beyond this life as well. Just as some people's personalities, lifestyles, and interests complement each other, there are combinations of personalities that clash and repel one another. It's Mother Nature's little joke that sometimes sexual attraction overrules common sense and instincts and we think we must have the very person who is the worst choice for us. Fight against the urge to bow to your libido. Make an informed choice. Know which person you are dealing with before jumping into intimacy. A baby that can be made in an instant will bind you together for the rest of your lives. Marriages can be dissolved. Shared parenthood cannot.

Want a glimpse into the future? Look at her parents. Unless she's adopted, she'll almost certainly adopt one or more of the stronger traits of either her mother or her father. You've heard the old wives' tale that all women turn into their mothers. It's still a wives' tale because women don't always grow into their mothers; sometimes they grow into their fathers. No, she probably won't grow a beard or ignore you in favor of the football game on TV, but her personality can just as easily mimic her father as her mother, or it may be a combination of both. You can usually determine which it is by paying close attention. At the very least, you'll have her parents in your life for their lifetimes. If these are not people you would care to spend your weekends and holidays with, then you might do well to pass on the daughter, too. Oh, and in these days of mix-and-match parents, make sure you're meeting the biological parents. In the nature versus nurture debate, I'm convinced nature wins.

One more comment on the subject of your perfect mate. If this woman is not a match for you, it isn't an insult to her or her parents. There is someone out there who fits into her family perfectly. It just isn't you. I know it sounds like a trite break-up line, but it is a truth. The thickness, length, thread style, and head size of a screw all must be right for it to fit into a machined hole. Otherwise, it won't go in at all or it will destroy the hole. Life is like that, too. It obeys physical laws. If it's right, you'll know it.

Chapter 14.
Knowledge is Power; More is Better

Knowledge is power. Just because there's nothing you can or should do with it at the moment doesn't mean you shouldn't notice and soak up all the knowledge available to you in the now. Knowing what's happening now gives you the basis you'll need for making decisions in the future. Keep your eyes open, learn, and remember. Every morsel of knowledge that crosses your path contributes to the whole of your wisdom.

When I was in college circumstances forced me to move to another part of the state after my third year in engineering school. The university I moved to declined to accept many of the classes I had already completed and my degree was delayed while I re-took those classes and completed a few others required by the new school but not the old. This, combined with my initial indecision in declaring a major, resulted in my graduation with almost 30 percent more credits than needed for the bachelor's degree in electrical engineering I was eventually awarded.

At the time, I was frustrated that it took six years to earn a four-year degree. Today I consider it a blessing. My false starts majoring in psychology, English, and mathematics provided me with insights into those disciplines that I might never have found had I majored in engineering from beginning to end. The "extra" engineering classes I was forced to take when the second university didn't recognize the first university's curriculum reinforced my understanding of those subjects.

My love of the English language and the mysteries of the human psyche continue to play a large role in my life. The knowledge I gleaned from the classes I completed in those arenas fused with my studies in the sciences of mathematics, physics, chemistry, and electricity to produce an outlook completely distinct from any one of those disciplines, yet synergistic of all. I feel very fortunate.

The moral of this story: No learning is ever wasted.

Chapter 15.
Don't Ever Stop Learning

Education continues throughout your lifetime. You finish high school, you finish college, you may even snag a graduate degree. The more you learn, the more you realize the body of knowledge you don't even know exists remains vast. This is a good sign, because the person who thinks he knows everything can learn nothing. Yes, it's another trite quip but nonetheless it's truth.

Keep your mind sharp by continuing to learn. You're never too old or too knowledgeable to learn something, and the person next to you always knows something you don't. Try to learn something from everyone you meet. Everyone who arrives in your life is there for a reason. Sometimes the reason is obvious, sometimes you'll never know why your paths crossed.

There's a theory that if you find yourself drawn to a person, there's something you need to learn from him. A related theory says if the same person crosses your path repeatedly, there's something you need to learn from him, and he will keep crossing your path until you learn that something. I don't know if either theory has merit, but I do know that I have often found myself amazed at the coincidence of a seemingly random meeting.

For instance, I was flying home to be with my mother during her serious spinal surgery and I was very worried about the procedure. The woman sitting next to me on the airplane was very quiet. We hardly spoke at all the entire trip. Just before the plane landed, we began to talk. She was a surgical nurse. I confided the purpose for my trip. Not only did she know the reputation of the surgeon, she was familiar with the details of the surgery my mother was facing. She was extremely encouraging and set my mind at ease to a considerable degree.

I can't begin to estimate how many times over the years I've uttered the phrase "Small world!" or

"What a coincidence!". Some say there are no coincidences. I only know that I have learned much from strangers during chance encounters.

Chapter 16.
Only You Can Take Care of You

Only you can take care of yourself. Sure, you pay doctors to watch over your health, but they can only work with what you tell them and they don't normally spend a lot of time on it at that. There are some dedicated physicians out there and this doesn't apply to them, but many times if the solution isn't one that occurs to your doctor while you're sitting in front of him, it likely won't occur to him at all. For this reason, it is your responsibility to know yourself and take it upon yourself to research your problem. If the doctor's solution doesn't work, it's up to you to guide him to the correct diagnosis by clearly laying out your relevant symptoms and filtering out the noise.

The same applies to accountants. First of all, your accountant won't know about your deductions unless you are very clear about what you've spent. Next, there are lots of tax laws out there and you should consider yourself awfully lucky if you find a truly gifted accountant who knows them all. If your situation isn't the "norm", you would be best served to research your own questions and find answers to them. If your circumstances require an accountant, by all means ask him your question. But if his answer doesn't sound right, ask another accountant. Just be aware that you know your own business best, and your business is not as important to anyone as it is to you.

Take care of yourself. Yes, there's lots to do to maintain a life. Lots and lots of little tasks—they overwhelm. But know that the one most important thing you can take care of, the one thing that cannot be slighted, is your mental and emotional well-being. Your life's purpose requires you to be joyful. Do what it takes to live joyfully. Experiencing joy is not a selfish extravagance, but rather it is necessary to healthy living. Without joy, you are not living, you are only existing. Don't read this as a stale commercial. Understand it, internalize it. To truly live, you must experience joy. Wake up from your mundane existence. Pursue joy. If you don't know what will bring you joy, meditate, ask your spirit guides. If you don't believe what they're telling you, ask for a sign. Red? You'll get the hang of it very quickly. Joy. Live with joy. Enjoy joy. Even in sadness and loss, the joy of living remains and supports you through the grief. When you live joyfully, your path guides you surely to your destination. Don't mistake joy for decadence; they are two entirely different things. Joy is productive; decadence is harmful. Yes, decadence sometimes is very clever at imitating joy. You'll know the difference, though. You're a smart kid.

Chapter 17.
Charity and Common Sense

Use common sense in giving. That's not to say you shouldn't help your friends. Of course you should! You should help strangers, too. It's good for your Karma. But look at the intention behind the request for help. Is the person asking for your help a manipulator? Will helping this person lead to inappropriate behavior on his or her part? Will this person make good use of your help? "Don't cast your pearls before swine," and "Help only the worthy," are difficult criteria to use as guidelines here. Who, after all, are we to judge who is worthy? But if you know the person who asks for your help will misuse your aid—that's an example of casting your pearls before swine and you shouldn't do it. Giving an addict money for his drug, whether it be cigarettes or something more dangerous and less legal, is a potentially volatile situation. Addicts are rarely sane when it comes to their addictions and you could be signing up for more than you bargained for. But to donate your hard-earned money to a person who simply doesn't work to make his own money because he prefers to live off the charity of others is a clear-cut case of casting your pearls before swine.

Of course, there could be a twist here, too. Perhaps that person is doing important work that doesn't carry a paycheck. Intent is the key and finding that key may be your responsibility. You can always ask the person how he intends to use the money. If it's an answer that indicates indolence, withhold the money and let the person hit up someone else.

There are so many people who do need and deserve your help! Giving your money to a parasite is almost sinful.

Chapter 18.
Don't Believe Everything You Read

Don't believe everything you read. Don't believe everything you hear, either. Most things have someone's spin on them, especially if that thing comes from the mass media like television, news, and magazines.

That's not to say the person making the statement is deliberately supplying false information. In some cases this is true, but in most instances he sincerely believes what he is saying. Or he's earning a really good living doing something he's really good at. It's called advertising. It's up to you to decode what is real and what is not. If you think one brand of toothpaste that costs more than another one will make your teeth whiter and your breath fresher, go ahead and try it. When you discover there's no difference, you can go back to the brand of toothpaste with the less exciting ad campaign.

One tenet of journalism places upon the reporter the responsibility to verify and confirm the statements he prints. This is a strictly observed rule in a responsible press. Sometimes, however, validity checks fall between the cracks and not-so-accurate information is published. Other times the press reporting the information is less than reputable and validity checks are bypassed in favor of spectacular, issue-selling, news. Then there's the just-plain-naïve communicator who believes what he's told regardless of the logic or the probability that his source is unreliable. Just as you must read the ingredients on the boxes of toothpaste to determine whether there's any difference in the two formulas, you must judge for yourself whether what you read in the press is truth or fiction.

Likewise, it's up to you to use what you read and what you hear as a starting point, and always leave open the possibility that there's another side to the story. News moguls are very good at second-guessing the decisions of our nation's leaders. I wonder how many of them would make better decisions if they were given the facts, all of the facts, upon which the decisions are based? It's certainly possible some of our leaders' decisions are ill-conceived. It is also possible that they are based on circumstances, events, and facts of which we have no knowledge.

Yes, lobbyists have great influence in our nation's capitol. I'm not suggesting political corruption doesn't exist. The point I'm trying to make is that much of the world's leadership happens behind closed doors. The most important contribution we can make is to elect honorable representatives whom we can trust to lead with integrity, and then allow them to do their jobs.

Recognize rabble-rousing for what it is and take no part in it. Acknowledge that all human beings have both good qualities and bad. No one is perfect. An elected official puts himself in the public eye, warts and all. If the wart doesn't interfere with his ability to do his job, leave it alone.

Chapter 19.
Map Your Spiritual Journey

There are many valid practices, doctrines, and methods for connecting with life. You don't have to master them all. You don't have to spend a week's salary or more learning how to practice a particular metaphysical art. There's nothing wrong with doing that, and if that is what you feel led to do, by all means do it. A spiritual teacher of old could find a patron who would support him and give him a livelihood. That isn't generally possible in today's society. Today's spiritual teacher must cobble together a living from multiple patrons.

Unfortunately, there are so many spiritual teachers out there that you can't support them all monetarily, nor is it in your best interest to try to learn all the different methods and teachings. You'd become fragmented and scattered if you attempted it. Concentrate on your talent, focus on what seems natural to you and leave the rest to others.

By the same token, there are many opportunists and charlatans ready to tell you anything you want to hear for a buck. Your job is to decipher which is legitimate and which is not. Just because everyone else is doing it doesn't make it right. Charismatic "teachers" can drum up tremendous followings and the collective energy of those believers works to make you think you're the only one who doesn't "get it". These fads don't last but while they're in fashion they can be costly in terms of money, lives and human suffering.

To complicate matters, your truth may be different from mine. I'm not talking about truth versus lie or black versus white. I'm talking about personal truth. At their foundations, our truths are the same, but the way truth manifests itself to you may be different than the way it manifests itself to me. That's why there are so many religions and denominations in the world—they're just different ways of looking at the same truth.

You'll know when you encounter it. Don't try to talk yourself into believing in anything that doesn't feel right to you. Recognition of truth can't be described, any more than love or beauty can be defined. You'll know love when you feel it, you'll know beauty when you see it, and you'll recognize your truth when you encounter it. It's as simple as that.

Chapter 20.
Pursue Your Life's Purpose

At some point in your life, you'll experience a physical reaction to something you learn or a revelation you have. In some people, this physical reaction triggers the sensation of goose bumps. For others, it's a feeling of sudden temperature change, physical movement, or a change in density in the air around them. For you, it may be something quite different. Whatever it is, this is your reaction to truth. Once you have experienced your truth, you'll have a frame of reference for the future and it will help you find your life's purpose.

Does everyone have a life's purpose? I don't know for certain but, yes, I think so. I certainly hope so, otherwise it's a great waste of time and a life. Does everyone find their life's purpose? No, definitely not. But I think to find and fulfill your life's purpose is the most rewarding achievement you could ask for. What is my life's purpose? For right now, I believe I know my life's purpose, but I haven't achieved it yet. I'll let you know on the flip side.

Sometimes people are given insight into their life's purpose but they don't pursue it because they're worried about what others will think. Don't worry about what other people think. This little pearl of wisdom comes from your grandmother as she approached her eightieth birthday:

> "When you get older, things fall into perspective. There are so many things I regret not having done. Just do what's in your heart and don't worry about what other people will think of you. If I hadn't spent so much of my life worrying about other people's opinions, I could look back on my life with a lot fewer regrets."

Most people have multiple life's purposes. For instance, a mother may know in her soul that she was brought into this world to bear and raise her child. But she may also have another purpose that she won't glimpse until her child is grown and her attention isn't focused on motherhood. And, remember, your life's purpose isn't necessarily the thing you do to earn money.

You aren't guaranteed to begin your life's work as soon as you've "completed" your educational training. Just as a child born prematurely usually experiences delayed physical development, so too can a soul become a "late bloomer". Delayed development does not mean a child is less intelligent. It simply means that she might experience milestones along a different timeline than might be expected to correlate to her birth date. For example, if a child was born three months prematurely and would have walked at twelve months had she been born at full term, she might be expected to walk at fifteen months due to her premature birth.

By the same token, an adult "late bloomer" can be thought of as being born years prematurely and might always feel years younger than his age, accomplishing certain milestones years after his peers accomplish them. I'm not saying he will attain maturity twenty years later, just that his physical age is running ahead of his spiritual timeline. He might feel he isn't "old enough" to do certain things when, in fact, he's plenty old enough, physically, mentally, and emotionally. He might spend the first twenty years of his adult life in a career that has nothing at all to do with his life's purpose, simply because he feels he's too young or not yet prepared.

One thing will be clear to you, though. If you are not working toward your life's purpose, you will be restless until you find it. Don't despair. You will recognize it when the time comes and once you've found it, you'll wonder what took you so long!

Chapter 21.
It's All About Me

People who came of age in the 1980s proudly proclaim, "It's all about me." They're not alone, though. Almost everyone is looking out for number one. It's sad, but true. Sometimes you'll find truly giving and altruistic people, but those saints are rare indeed. Maybe this will change as our collective consciousness is raised, but for now be aware of this truth. And be aware of it in yourself as well.

One reason this unattractive human trait is so prevalent is that we find it difficult to recognize in ourselves and so it is allowed to perpetuate. We don't distinguish between promoting ourselves and squashing everyone else. It's so easy to convince ourselves that our actions are for the best. The mother who is a homeless heroin addict and spends every cent she can scrape together on her drug doesn't turn her child over to someone else to raise because she tells herself she's a good mother and her love for her child and her child's love for her are all that matters. She doesn't foresee that she's raising a future drug addict, and if anyone tried to tell her that, she would not believe it. She is more concerned with her own perception of herself as a good mother than with her child's welfare, even as she loves the child with all her being.

Now don't take this to mean that mothers with low incomes should give their children away! That's not at all what I'm saying and you know it. A child who watches her mother inject drugs into her veins, or endures the altered personality of her drug-influenced mother is being mentally and emotionally abused by the person who loves her best in the world, a person who would passionately argue that she is a good mother. That is a far cry from a child who wears secondhand clothes and lives in low-income housing.

Since these misguided souls truly believe their actions are for the best, sometimes you must look closely to recognize your nemesis. The co-worker who sees you as competition might convince himself that you're bad for the company and blacken your name behind your back in an effort to have you fired. Every time anything goes wrong, he'll insist to all who will listen that it was your fault. You'll be asked to leave and never know why. Or maybe you will know why, but you'll be powerless to stop it because, by that time, the "awareness" of your incompetence has become so deep-seated that no one will question its truth. Yes, this is an extreme example of an overly inflated ego, but this person is common enough that you'll see it in more workplaces than not.

When you feel you have been wronged, look closely. Often, you'll discover someone taking the "look out for number one" rule just a bit too far. People are rarely motivated by pure malice. We can usually convince ourselves we are justified in our actions if we work on it long enough and hard enough.

Unfortunately, many are adept at this self-deception and conduct their lives by tearing others down. They make themselves bigger and more important in their own minds by making the rest of us smaller.

Some are so good at it that they can go for many years before their motives are recognized.

It may appear that these people always win. That's okay. Truly, they will reap as they have sown. The Golden Rule will catch up with them. Karma always does. Their actions will, at some point, come back to them.

Take care of your own Karma and let others do the same. Don't help them to damage you by entertaining bitterness or resentment against them. That internal resentment hurts only you, certainly not them. You want to minimize the damage to yourself and you do that by accepting that it happened, let the laws of nature take care of retribution, and look around for the opportunity the change in your circumstances offers you.

If you focus on revenge, anger, hurt, or any other negative emotion, you will only draw more of that same negative energy to yourself. Let it go, know that everything happens for a reason, and that it's your job to see the good fortune the seemingly negative event brings to you.

This does not mean you should consciously allow yourself to be wronged. Just be aware that in financial transactions it's almost always every man for himself. Sometimes you'll be lucky and the person on the other side of your business transaction will be ethical. Other times, you'll have to insist on receiving value for your money.

Remember, too, that the opposite is also true. When you are hired to work for someone, that someone is paying you to further his interests, not your own. You may at times disagree with the person signing your paycheck and it is permissible and right that you express your thoughts and opinions if that is what you are being paid to do. There is a fine line, though, at which offering well-meaning advice morphs into self-serving manipulation.

Strive to remember you are there to assist and contribute to the boss' success. If your opinions and his don't match, you can do one of two things. You can offer your thoughts and then do all in your power to help him achieve his goals whether they are in accordance with your views or not, or you can find another job. Do not fall into the trap of rationalizing that you know best to justify marshalling events and circumstances in opposition to your employer's goals and in support of your own. Again with the Golden Rule: Do unto your employer as you would have your employee do unto you.

Chapter 22.
Keep Your Goat Hidden

One way advertising agencies sell products is by tapping into our emotions—love, envy, sex, and guilt are biggies. Some people use similar methods of gaining control over us by triggering our anger. They know instinctively that if they can make us angry enough, we won't think clearly and they'll have a better chance of manipulating us. One way to protect yourself from this sort of manipulation is to keep your buttons, or your goat, hidden. If they don't know you are likely to explode with anger when treated with disrespect, they're less likely to use that tactic to distract and manipulate you. It's the same concept used by athletes since time out of mind. Anger the competition and he loses focus and you gain the advantage.

Some people are very good at manipulating others through emotions. It's almost as if they can feel what the other person feels. They know instinctively what to say or do to generate intense emotions in their victims and they don't hesitate to use that knowledge to the fullest extent. The person with this ability is generally a very good salesperson and your best defense is to keep your poker face intact and run fast and far when you find yourself targeted.

Another valuable benefit to governing your negative emotions harkens back to an earlier chapter, The Art and Science of Life. Not only are you protecting yourself from manipulation, but you aren't contributing noxious emotions to your environment and mine. Your body doesn't experience the stress of intense negative emotions. Your reasoning remains cool and logical. The people around you aren't exposed to negativity and stress. Everybody except the manipulator wins. When you pull this one off, you are the hero.

Chapter 23.

Be True to Yourself

If it feels wrong, don't do it. Trust your instincts. It's as simple as that. Hoards of people may clamor for you to do what you know in your heart is wrong. They'll twist facts and spin stories until you're exhausted trying to untangle the truth from the lies. Whether your mind can pinpoint the flaw in the logic or not, your gut will know the truth. Trust it. Of all the folks out there looking out for number one, some are dishonest and will leave you holding the bag if it means a small gain for them. Too many folks are out for their own self-interests (everyone else be damned!). They will do everything in their power to lead you in the wrong direction. Use your moral compass, my son, and don't be led astray.

A realtor recently gave me an explanation for why it's okay to commit mortgage fraud. Obviously, she had a commission on the line and she was determined to collect it, regardless of the position it left me in. She said:

> "It's illegal to jaywalk, but people do it. It's illegal to speed, but people do that, too. Sometimes they get caught; sometimes they don't. If you provide a fake document in order to get a loan, it's likely nobody will ever know it."

Nobody but me, the realtor, and the crooked loan officer, that is. Obviously, I didn't fall for her logic—I certainly wouldn't be advertising it here if I did! Many people have fallen for this line and similar ones, however. The economic meltdown suffered by our country and the world was a direct result of this particular flavor of dishonesty.

Make it your goal to live your life in such a way that you have nothing to hide. Behave as if you were preparing to become a politician and wanted to leave no skeletons in your closet for the opposition to rattle. If you want to play, be prepared to pay, because eventually the game will end and all obligations will have to be settled. Very few are fortunate enough or pure enough to leave the table with no moral or ethical debts to pay, but if you play your cards right, you get to keep your soul.

About the Author

FANNY WEBB is a mother, a grandmother and a perpetual student. She lives in coastal Virginia where she continues daily to observe and learn new lessons through her own experiences and through the eyes of her offspring.

PENNY TRAIL PRESS

P. O. Box 2712

Virginia Beach, Virginia 23450

USA

To order copies of this publication, visit us at

www.pennytrailpress.com

or email

info@pennytrailpress.com

www.ingramcontent.com/pod-product-compliance
Lightning Source LLC
Chambersburg PA
CBHW051807040426
42446CB00007B/552